Memoirs of
A Child in Poole

Mary Louisa Fisher

Edited, designed and prepared for publication by Suzannah Trickett.

Photographs (except where indicated) and content by Mary Louisa Fisher.

No part of this publication may be reproduced, stored in a retrieval system or transmitted in any form or by any means, electronic, mechanical, photocopying, recording or otherwise, without the prior permission of the publisher and copyright holder.

Front cover:
The Guildhall, Market Street, Poole.

Back cover:
Photograph taken by Suzannah Trickett on board "Glory Be" at Old Harry Rocks.

All enquiries to; Suzannah Trickett – artisanfoodie@yahoo.co.uk

Copyright © 2018 Mary Louisa Fisher

All rights reserved.

ISBN: 172746799X
ISBN-13: 978 - 1727467994

Acknowledgements

The author wishes to thank her daughter Suzannah, the designer, for all her help in putting this book together and is extremely grateful for all of her efforts in delivering my memories so expeditiously.

The author and designer wish to express their thanks and gratitude to the staff at The Poole Museum Service and Scaplen's Court for the loan of prints and photographs and all other assistance acquired for the purpose of this publication.

Conversion - 12d = 1 shilling 1/- = 5p

Contents

Preface 5

The Changes 6

    These Changes 6

Heritage 6

Wartime 1939 - 1945

My Birth 8

The House 8

    The Lavatory 13

    The Bedrooms 13

    Our Room 14

    Our Bed 14

    The Box Room 14

    Lighting 15

    The Sitting Room 15

    The Scullery 17

    No Washing Machines 20

    The Ironing 21

    The Pantry 22

Lagland Street County Primary (Infant) School 23

Clothes 23

1945 - 1950 (End of War)

- The Men 24
- The Slums of Poole 26
- The Demolition 26
    - The Split Up 26
    - The Move 27
    - The Workhouse 27
- St James Church 27
- South Road Junior Mixed School 29
- School Dinners 29
- Playtime 32
- Sunday School 34
- The Women 35
- Our New House 36
    - The Inside 36
    - The Accommodation 37
- It's Getting Better 40
- Ration Books 41
    - Swapping 41
- Growing up in Poole 41
- My Gran 42
- Gran's House 42
- The Visits 44
- The Cottage Garden 44
- The Women of Poole 45
- The Community 46

Mrs Toms	46
The Coal Man	46
The Weekly Shop	47
The Butchers	48
The Bakers	48
The Fishmongers	48
Millers Pie Shop	49
The Chemist	49
The Grocery Shops	49
The Shoe Shop	49
The Sweet Shop	49
The Ice Cream Man	50
The Fishing Boats	50
Clothes Shops	50
The Railway Box	51
The Greengrocer	51
The Pubs	52
The Pub Run	52
Christmas Time 1946-1950	55
My Grandparents	58

Changes & Conclusion

Baiter	59
Changes to Poole	62

The Swimming Baths 67
Poole Park 67
A Change for the Better 67
A Good Change 67
Other Good changes. 69

My Conclusion – At least for now. 71

Preface

*I*t was a beautiful sunny day walking along the quayside at the stunning Poole Harbour. I stopped to take a break and while sitting on a bench I engaged in an insightful conversation with an older woman of Poole whom was born in Market Street.

During our conversation, *simply* spoken to me were her words:-

"They are making our Poole a concrete jungle"

These words resonated with me and made me open my eyes to taking a good look around. As a subsequence, I became overwhelmed with the memories of my childhood as I walked those streets of Poole. I began reminiscing about the wonderful times, some good and some bad.

It became very clear to me of how Poole has changed so dramatically today. I wanted to share my memories; my thoughts and feelings; my experiences; and to document, not only my opinion of Poole now, but for historical reasons too, regarding that period of my life, which means so very much to me.

This book is short stories, an insight, on what life was like as a child growing up in Poole during and after the Second World War for the period of 1940 – 1950.

The Changes

Poole has seen many changes leading right back to its very beginning.

Moreover, during the last century, I have been witness to many of these changes, the good and the bad.

I now feel that I would like to share those times with you before most of the original people of Poole leave it, and, who like me, are still interested in the development of our town.

Looking around I can see that there are still ongoing changes taking place at this very moment in time, 2018 and more to come, and I am wondering what Poole will look like for our future generations?

These Changes

For whom are they going to be? Moreover, will these changes be for the better or for the worse for Poole?

Heritage

I came from a long line of Poole people, many generations of master mariners, blacksmiths and fishermen (Anglers). My grandfather was in the navy at one time, therefore I have always had a strong connection with Poole Harbour and the sea. My son Robert has inherited the love of the sea and Poole bay. Whenever he can, he will be out on the water in his boat "Glory Be".

My son Robert, fishing along the Jurassic Coast on his boat "Glory Be" accompanied by one of my daughters, Angela – 2017.

"Glory Be" 2018.

Wartime 1939-1945

My Birth

I was born at home in 1940 at Lake Road, Hamworthy. It was in temporary accommodation, a prefab I believe, as it was at the beginning of the Second World War (1939-1945). We were quite a large family then. Shortly after my birth, we moved to Green Lane, Poole where my mother later had another baby girl, making us a grand family of eight.

The House

*T*his was a rented house as most of the houses in Poole at that time were. I can still remember this time very clearly.

The house was very small, two up and two down, no front door only a back entrance. We had no bathroom to speak of; instead, hung up on the fence in the yard outside, you would find a long tin bath, which we used for bathing.

Friday night was bath time, and two of us young girls had to bathe together in the scullery or in front of the fire during the cold winter months. Our mother used to scrub us with Lifebuoy Carbolic soap; the same soap that she scrubbed the scullery floor with, it did not do us any harm. The scented one came later. My two eldest sisters used to go to The Bath House at The Guildhall in Market Street, Poole. You had to take your own towel and pay a penny for hot water and soap.

Green Lane – source; The Poole Museum.

This is where our house would have stood today – 2018.

The Guildhall, Market Street – 2018 (front cover).
Now Poole Registry Office.

*Side elevation of The Guildhall – 2018.
The ground floor is where the bathing took place.*

The Lavatory

I remember it well! It was down the bottom of the yard. The lavatory seat was wooden, long, wide and green with a hole in the middle for a clay pot. It was a little high for me. The chain was a Victorian pulley one, which it made a hell of a noise when flushing. Torn pieces of newspaper, draped over a piece of string tied between two nails, were there to use. After the war, we had Izal toilet paper. Izal toilet paper was exactly that, paper! With a slightly abrasive surface and contained germicide for hygiene. Nothing like the soft toilet rolls which we have today. I must say it was not much better than the newspaper though, Oh, happy days. When it was getting dark, I used to ask one of my sisters to take me down the path, as I was only little and a bit frightened of the dark. We were a very close family and took care of one another.

The Bedrooms

*O*ur parents had a room of their own, which was at the front of the house, facing the lane outside. They had a big brass metal bed with both knobs on the headrail and the bottom rail at the foot of the bed. I used to enjoy unscrewing these knobs, much to the annoyance of my mother. The base had many springs in it that required regular dusting. I liked springing up and down on it to see how high I could go. I never did reach the ceiling. Inherited from my mother's mother Alice Bridle and her father Robert Bridle, was also a large wardrobe made from walnut and a dressing table with a triple mirror upon it and beneath it, two draws and cupboards. On the top of the dressing table, there was a diamond-shaped tray made from glass, with a glass ring holder, but I never did see any rings on it. In my mother's lifetime, she only owned a wedding ring, which she wore all of the time. In the wardrobe, hung up, was a black Charleston dress, very 1930's, with tassels above the knees. I used to put it on and enjoyed swinging it about. Of course, it came down to my ankles. There was also a pair of platform shoes, much too big for me, although my mother was only a small Poole woman, as many Poole people were; I believe she was a shoe size 3. Today that dress would be Vintage now!

There was a very long trunk in their room and on the bed was a striped bolster that went right across the bed. Nowadays, the pillow supersedes Bolsters. Of course, a real cotton sheet, which required ironing, none of the polyester you see today and a candlewick quilt completes the bedding. My baby sister slept in their room, more than likely, in a large draw as they did in those times.

Our Room

I had to share a room and the bed with three of my older sisters. Two up top and two at the foot of the bed and in the morning I usually ended up with someone's feet on my pillow. Looking out from our bedroom window, I can remember counting the coal buckets that went back and forth, up high across Green Road from the quayside to Pitwinnes and back. Some people count sheep to get to sleep, I used to count buckets. On occasion, we would sleep in the downstairs front room under a metal Morrison shelter to protect us; it could fit a double bed!

Our Bed

*O*ur bed was made of black wrought iron, very plain. The mattress was very lumpy, filled with wadding I expect. For bed linen, there was a cotton sheet, an itchy blanket, a quilt and my father's heavy long coat to keep us warm in the winter and sometimes a china hot water bottle. There were fireplaces in each of the bedrooms which could be lit in the case that anyone was ill. Put underneath our bed, was an enamel pot in case you needed to go to the loo during the night.

The Box Room

*I*t was small and our only brother's bedroom. We also used it as our playroom. I can remember one time, coming up to May Day, helping my brother and sister make a Maypole in the box room, for us to dance around in the street lanes on May Day for pennies. Nothing posh though more than likely an old broom handle and some paper ribbons to make it look pretty.

Lighting

We had gas in the house. Our lighting was by mantles, which were very fragile and broke very easily if you touched them while you were lighting the globes. At night, we went upstairs to bed with a lighted waxed candle in a candlestick. Talk about the nursery rhyme "Wee Willie Winkie runs through the town, upstairs and downstairs in his nightgown". Also fuelled by gas, were the lamppost lanterns in the lane outside. Given that, it was wartime and for fear of invasion, the lanterns were not illuminated. I remember the lanes and roads being quite dark and seeing a man lighting the lamps from my gran's attic window after the war.

Example of the candlestick holders – On display at Scaplen's Court, Poole – 2018.

The Sitting Room

Had a black range with a fire grate and a mantle shelf, on which stood a clock that required manual winding, along with two copper vases. I remember my mother sitting in a chair by the fire. There was a long window in the room with no curtains; I expect they had to put something up to the window at night as a blackout during the war years. In the middle of the room stood a large wooden table made from pine with chairs, one had arms for father. A mahogany chest of drawers stood against the wall, it would have been worth quite a lot today, but sadly it was destined to be chopped up for firewood.

Example of a Range cooker – On display at Scaplen's Court, Poole– 2018.

The Scullery

Was small, it had whitewashed walls and our gas meter was high upon it by the back door that led to the yard. On two brick plinths, stood a shallow stone sink about 6" in depth; it had one tap, supplying cold water only, with a rubber squirter on it. Underneath the sink, stood a white enamel pail with a lid on the top containing a little bleach. We used the pail to empty the pots from our bedrooms in the mornings. This was the only sink in our house! The mind boggles. How did my mother manage with us all, with my dad and five children and a baby to look after? By hard graft, that is how. Carried out by hand was the cleaning of all of our laundry. My mother used Persil and blue bag rinse for the whites. No disposable nappies in those days, only "Terry Towelling" nappies that were also hand washed, but boiled upon the stove first in a dedicated white enamel pail. As a young girl my mother worked at The White House Laundry in Poole, so she certainly gained a lot of training and knowledge in the cleaning of laundry items.

The scullery had a small wooden pine table with a drawer, which is where we kept the cutlery. Next to the table there was a stool, on which stood the enamel bowls for washing and washing up. Mother used soda crystals for this and a little mop on a stick. In the corner stood a black painted cupboard with a drawer where we kept the cooking spoons etc. Inside the cupboard was things like; Jeyes fluid, bleach, soda, toilet soap and soap powder, no liquid in those days; After the war came Lux soap flakes that were used for woollens and delicate fabrics, not nylon, polyester or acrylics. Soap bars – Sunlight and Lifebuoy; polishes for the boots and shoes; and Brasso used for cleaning and polishing of the copper pots and Windowlene for the windows. I loved the smell of that cupboard I can still smell it today. There was also a chair and on it stood a box full of potatoes with the dirt still on them and a shopping bag.

Example of our scullery (1) – On display at Scaplen's Court, Poole – 2018.

Example of our scullery (2) – On display at Scaplen's Court, Poole – 2018.

No Washing Machines

Everything was soaked overnight in enamel bowls with hot boiled water and added Persil. Then scrubbed by hand in the morning and rinsed in cold water. My mother starched my father's shirt collars using Robin's powdered starch, none of the fancy sprays were around then. My mother rung out all of the washing by hand and then put the items through the mangle, which stood outside by the back door. We had a pulley washing line, which squeaked when it was moving. My mother would peg the laundry onto the washing line using wooden pegs, which flew high in the wind. Sometimes when bringing in the washing, it had smuts from the smoking chimneys on them.

Example of our mangle – On display at Scaplen's Court, Poole – 2018.

The Ironing

Using the sitting room table instead of an ironing board, Mother would place the items requiring ironing, on old clean blankets, with remnants of some scorch marks on them. There was an iron metal stand, but sometimes the iron would slip off. To heat the iron my mother used to place it directly on top of the gas flame on the gas cooker. If there were not enough pennies for the gas, Mother would place the iron directly on the flat top of the hot range plate, fuelled by coal or coke. Along with the iron used to sit our heavy black iron kettle. They always used a potholder to pick up the iron. Around the range was a fireguard with a brass edging which reached very hot temperatures. Mother sometimes put my father's things (clothing) on it to air, although we did have a wooden clotheshorse too. The cooking pots were black heavy cast iron, but we did have some enamel saucepans hung on the walls along with cups, plates and bowls in the pantry.

An example of the type of iron and clotheshorse we had used. Both items on display at Scaplen's Court, Poole – 2018.

The Pantry

No fridge and no electricity! The Pantry did not contain much, built under the stairs with a door off the sitting room. There were some shelves and a sloping ceiling. The pantry contained the usual basic things like loose tea in a tin, no tea bags in those days; sugar; Bev and Camp liquid coffee; cocoa; Daddies sauce and porridge oats, which Mother made every morning with water to fill us up. I still love it and have porridge for my breakfast daily, but made with milk now, be it winter or summer. There was also an old empty Smith's crisp tin for the bread, if we were lucky. Bread was unsliced and unwrapped in those days. A brown ceramic teapot covered with a leather tea cosy and a stainless steel tea strainer stood on a shelf. The wooden shelves had hooks screwed into the wood all along it, for the cups, jugs etc. to hang on.

However, we did get national dried milk for babies and bottled orange juice that you added water to, from the government. Typically, on a Sunday, Dad would cook up a cabbage. Dad used to line us up to drink the cooking water instead of pouring it down the sink. He said it was good for us, but thinking about it now, I would say, possibly good by way of health benefits, but the amount of salt used in cooking in those days was colossal, so I think our salt intake would have been through the roof! He also made a large bread pudding with any stale bread or crust. Now there is a laugh! It was wartime and you had to queue half way down the high street from "Hoares" the bakery for a loaf, but we did have it sometimes to fill us up. He put some spice in it and a little of dried fruit with a bit of marg (margarine) and an egg or dried egg. It was delicious and smelt lovely, but when you are hungry, and which we always were, anything and everything does. My father used to bring home a rabbit on occasion. Something which he; hung, skinned and made into rabbit stew for the family, delicious and warming on a cold winters day.

When my gran made an apple pie with apples from the tree in her garden, only a small tree, she sent the apple peel wrapped in newspaper, around to our house for us children to eat. Now there is poverty for you! Nevertheless, she did teach me at a young age how to make wonderful apple pies and pastry, and my son and daughter's say, "They are the best ever".

Lagland Street County Primary (Infant) School

I attended at four years old I believe. I can remember the bomb shelters in the playground. When the sirens went off, us children went running like the clackers to the bomb shelters with our gas mask on. We would have to sit and wait on the benches inside until we received the "all clear" and then we proceeded back inside the classroom. At playtimes, we received a small "free" bottle of milk, cod liver oil, and malt if you were skinny. We all were, and I still am.

Clothes

*W*e all had clothing coupons during the war years, so you could not go out and buy what you needed, even if you had the money to do so. It was "make" or "mend", this meant that you had to look after your clothes. I usually got "hand me downs", no pretty frocks (dresses) and my shoes did not fit me properly and hurt my two little toes. Nevertheless, I had to wear them, or I had to go barefoot, which I often did in the summertime. I remember wearing shoes to school with holes in the bottoms, lined with cardboard, often from used cereal boxes. Quite funny when you think back, as I can remember lifting my feet up and you could read Kellogg's on the bottom of your shoes, but there was no shame. I had friends that came from much larger families of 8-12 children, so we were all in the same boat so to speak. If you got a brand new pair of shoes, or boots (for the boys) studs, known as Blakey's, were put in the bottom of them to make them last longer and what a noise they made on the flagstone pavements!

1945-1950 (End of War)

The Men

*I*n those days, young or older men wore hats or caps if they worked on the quay. A collarless shirt with usually the sleeves rolled up, dark coloured trousers with a pair of braces and a wide leather belt. Black boots with studs in the bottoms, which made a clip-clop sound along the path when walking home after a long hard day's work. Usually, dinner was on the table ready for them. Then the fun begins, with the wife washing his back at the scullery sink. The husband did the rest, by soaking his feet in a bowl of hot soapy water.

The fishermen wore dungarees and a polo neck navy blue jumper to keep out the cold, and oilskins to keep them dry, with a thick woollen hat and boots. As he had once been in the navy, my grandfather wore black boots that he polished with Black Cherry Blossom boot polish or Kiwi. You could see your face in them. He also smoked a pipe.

My father did not work on the quay and as such, he wore shirts with removable collars that my mother used to wash and then starch. My mother polished my father's boots too with a high glistening shine and as always, he wore a cap. My father did not smoke but took a pinch of snuff, he liked a beer, but I never saw him drunk, after all, he was head of the family. My how things have changed!

At the outset of the war, Sir Winston Churchill, then first Lord of The Admiralty, insisted that the Royal Navy must have its own independent supply of Cordite, a mixture of nitro-glycerine and gun cotton. The chosen site for the new Cordite factory was at Holton Heath, which was 4 miles from Poole. It opened in early 1916 and drew heavily on Poole for its workforce one of which was my father. It was then essential to produce adequate quantities of acetone whose solvent action assisted the incorporation of the nitro-glycerine with the gun cotton.

*My father, Harold Frederick Fisher.
After having received an award for his long time in service at the Cordite factory – 1960.*

The Slums of Poole

Poole had a terrible housing crisis, with overcrowding in every street. The problem was money! There was not any! I would like to say that we did not live in these conditions because my father was lazy or unemployed; it was because my father was poorly paid! He worked very hard and tried to support his family. There was not any help from the government, and certainly no family allowance back then. If you did not work, you had no money, simple! So why should they move out of Poole?

My parents Harold and Ethel Fisher were both born in Poole. The Fishers of Poole go back many generations, but my mother's father Robert Bridle (my grandfather) was born in Sydling St Nicholas, Dorset. My great grandparents, Charles and Jane Bridle, moved to Poole when my grandfather was aged two. My mother's mother was a Brown, another old Poole family name.

The Demolition

The Poole Council said all the houses in our lane had to be demolished because they would cost too much to repair and the property owners/landlords were not willing to help with the costs of the repairs. They were not fit for human habitation, and they had to go. This meant we had to find somewhere else to live. Given that we were a large family, it was not an option for all of us to stay together whilst we searched for new accommodation. Therefore, sadly the family had to be split up whilst my father sought a new home for us all.

The Split Up

My father went to stay at his mother and father's house nearby in Poole with my twelve-year-old sister so that he could continue to work and my sister could go to school. Gran still had my uncle Harry Fisher living at her home, my dad's eldest brother, so she did not have enough room for all of us.

The Move

It took about 6 months for my father to find us a new home, a definitive change for the better. But during this time, we lost our community of Poole that we had become accustomed too.

The Workhouse

My mother; my eldest sister, then aged 13; the three of us younger children and my youngest sister, who was a toddler, all went into the workhouse at Sturminster Newton in Dorset, it was 1946. This was a very hard time for my mother, as not only had our family gone through the separation, but also because her grandmother died in the workhouse and my mother feared that she would never leave, as many women did not. Even now, my eldest sister rarely will talk about this. Workhouses were a place that you would go to if you were destitute and had no money. Thankfully, we only stayed for six months or so. My father and sister came to visit us at The Workhouse during the weekends and the wardens used to line us up for them to see us. Years later, my sister told me that she could never get over how clean we looked.

St James Church

They christened my two eldest sisters at St James Church. Gran made sure of this. She was a member of the church, a very Christian woman and did a lot to help the church. On a brass plate inside the church, up on the wall, is her sons' name, Ernest Fisher. My uncle Ernest died at only 19 years old in the Great War (1914-1918) and he was laid to rest at the Tynecot Cemetery in Belgium.

Her mother, Agnes Bartlett (maiden name) a fishmonger, was married to George Manfred Grant a shoemaker, in St James Church. But my grandad, Harry John Fisher, who was a mariner, married her in St Pauls (now demolished), in the High Street Poole, as was my mothers' parents, family name Bridle.

St James Church – 2018.

South Road Junior Mixed School

My two eldest sisters first went to Lagland Street School (also known as Rattrays), and then went on to St James Sabbath Church School in Church Street. During the Second World War, a bomb hit St James Sabbath Church School, and during this time, they temporarily went to Lagland Street School (now demolished and flats lay where the school once stood).

For a while, I went to South Road Junior Mixed School, I loved it there. The head was Mr Hartnell. He was very jolly and round in stature. My teacher was Mr Francis, he was a very nice man, my friends and I used to take great pleasure in teasing him for fun. Good job he had a sense of humour. On May Day, we had a very large Maypole in the playground, full of long ribbons. We each held one, our class, girls and boys, danced around it to music, going in and out, as we skipped around, up and down. Oh, happy days!

School Dinners

I remember after the war, at the end of South Road, on the corner of Lagland Street, there was a white prefab looking building which is where the school dinners were prepared. This site now houses a block of council flats. In early 1945, work commenced for the preparation for provision of school midday meals at South Road Junior Mixed School, which is when the "Meals in Schools" scheme started on the premises. I can see myself taking a plate and queuing in a long line of schoolchildren. The dinner ladies stood behind the food as we all ushered along quickly. We had two choices, you take it, or you leave it. The dinner ladies would fill up your plate. We always had mashed potato, that was lumpy on occasion and some stew like offering, accompanied with glorious cabbage at the majority of meal times. Sometimes we had fish. Nevertheless, whatever we had, it was hot and filled us up. When your plate was loaded up, you went off to sit at a table on a bench seat. In the middle of the table was a large jug of gravy, Ah bisto! A lifesaver! As if the meal was, shall we say politely, less appetising, then you would swamp your food to make it more edible.

I particularly looked forward to puddings mostly at school mealtimes. Hot strawberry jam tart…. Mmm Yum! The puddings were served from a large silver metal tray. The dinner lady used to cut a square piece of tart from the tray, place it in a bowl and then pour all over the luscious hot custard, served from a large enamel jug, delicious! Sometimes we had hot chocolate sponge with chocolate custard, red jelly or pink blancmange, and then there was semolina with a nice spoonful of strawberry jam. Of course, I cannot leave out Sago or Tapioca, YUK! We used to call it frogspawn! On other days, we would have rice pudding or macaroni, lovely jubbly! I used to think we were the unfortunate ones when it came to school dinners, but seeing what the children are eating today, now I am not so sure.

South Road Junior Mixed School – 2018.
Now aptly named "Poole Old Town Infant School & Nursery.

St James Sabbath Church School – 2018.

Playtime

School playtime was wonderful; first, there would be skipping ropes that whacked the ground as you sung or a shorter one that you used to do "the bumps". Next, would come spinning tops, all colours, all sizes with a whip made from a leather bootlace on a stick. How it did crack! Cost you all of your pocket money, about sixpence. There would be ball "upsys" games, marbles or alleys (as they were then called) there were dibs, leapfrog and hopscotch on the paths. All we needed was a piece of white chalk from school, and of course, not forgetting, the notable conkers, tied on by a leather bootlace.

As I write about conkers, I remembered recently taking a short break in beautiful Devon where one of my daughters lives. I decided to go for a walk; my grandson Jaxson who was nine years old at the time asked if he could join me. I said "yes" and off we went heading down the bridle path. Spotting a tree covered in very prickly conkers, with a stick, I managed to knock some down. We broke them open; they were big, brown and shiny. Jaxson was very pleased. I said, "You will be able to play conkers with your friends at school now Jaxson". Jaxson's reply to me was "Oh no Nanny, we cannot take them to school, we are not allowed". I was most disappointed with his reply, and thinking, my, how things have changed. We carried on with our walk abiding by the country codes by shutting the gates behind us as we went. There were many sheep in the fields and a large hare ran out in front of us, which startled us both. Jaxson picked a few wildflowers for his mummy and when we reached the top of the hill, he said, "We are on top of the world" I replied, "yes, that we are Jaxson".

My grandson, Jaxson – 2015.

Sunday School

We had to attend Sunday school our Gran said so. Your grandparents were heavily involved within your family life. They had their say and going to Sunday school was one of them. We always wore our "best clothing", adults and children alike. This clothing was kept only for Sunday's and special occasions. You always had a nice coat and hat, usually, a Kangol Beret made from wool, with matching gloves and your best Clark's shoes. At Easter time, we wore Easter Bonnets all covered in flowers mine was lemon. It is still my favourite colour. My sisters wore pink and we all had a little bag of almond paste to take home with us.

Mount Street Hall, where I attended Sunday school – 2018.

The Women

Wore silver colour metallic curlers covered with a turban in their hair during the day because it was hard to sleep with them in throughout the night. They even went to the corner shop like this along with their crossover aprons, generally with a flower pattern on them. In the 1945-1950's, there was not a lot of toiletries around for women in those days to enable them to make themselves look pretty for the men in their lives. Nevertheless, there was a powdered shampoo called Palmolive and a liquid pouch called Silverkrin that made their hair look soft and shiny. A secret was, if you were a blonde-haired woman, you would put a spot of lemon juice in your last "cold" rinse to make it shine. However, if you were a brunette-haired woman, you would add a little vinegar to your last rinse, for the same reason. For scent, there were toilets soaps like Pears, Lux, Palmolive, Knights Castile and Lifebuoy.

I can remember my gran saying, "a lady never wears trousers" and certainly not jeans! Considered as "common" you would have been known as, if you did so. They are for working men," she would say. I was growing up and I believed her then. I now have at least 12 pairs in my wardrobe. Which brings to my mind a book by Catherine Cookson called "Colour Blind," it was very true even at this time, but how things have changed!

Fashion came later! With stockings, if you were lucky enough to own any. The stockings had black seems running up the back of them. Do you remember girls? No tights only suspender belts then; if you had a tummy you wore "roll-ons" For those that had a boyfriend in the services; he would send them home to you. If not, then you had to draw one on your bare legs remembering to get it straight.

Then came split skirts and the swagger coat. Most young people were slim back then and the shops did not stock young clothes over a size 12. Very rarely did you see a large person. How things have changed regarding clothing sizes today!

Our New House

*N*ow, this was a change for the better. The house we moved into was a great improvement to the old one in Green Lane. I believe it was around 1947/8, a semi-detached house, which had a front garden and large back garden, severely overgrown. I can recall my father carrying me down the garden, because of all the prickles. There was a coalhouse and an outside lavatory joined onto the house, not down the end of the yard like before, and a little shed at the side. This time around, the house had a front and back door, with many windows.

The Inside

*J*ust bare wooden floorboards, no carpets at all! All the furniture from our old house was all inside; someone must have been storing it for us while we were away in *The Workhouse*. The table was a large old farmhouse style, given to my mother by a member of her family. I do not know whom. The table, constructed from pine with a scrubbable top, which my mother later changed to a wipeable pretty oilcloth. I recall my mother saying to me one day "I will chop it up for firewood." However, she never did, as we always needed the table. I can remember when I had a birthday I said to my father "can I have a party?" to which he replied, "There is a party every day in this house sat around that very table" and pointing to it as he spoke. He was right, as always, you never did question him. Once all of us six came and went, my parents, used the table for the following twenty grandchildren.

Times were still hard though, when we ran out of milk and sugar, in the pantry there was sometimes a tin of Nestles condensed milk. This we used to stir a teaspoon or so into a hot cup of tea or coffee, to give it colour and sweetness. On occasion, a good substitute for sugar was a spoonful of Tate and Lyle Golden Syrup, but alternatively we liked this spread onto bread and margarine when we ran out of cheap jam, usually the rhubarb and ginger variety. Other tinned food substitutes Mother relied upon in place of meat when she could not afford to buy it, was corned beef from Argentina and minced beef with onions. We usually ate these items cold with hot boiled potatoes accompanied by Marrowfat peas and Bisto gravy, made using the powdered variety, none of the instant gravies were around then. Anything to fill us kids up when we came in starving! We did have dried peas too, but they would need to be soaked overnight in water and then cooked the next day.

*Example of our farmhouse style kitchen table
On display at Scaplen's Court, Poole – 2018.*

The Accommodation

We now had electric and gas in this house with two-meter cupboards requiring a shilling at a time. The kitchen had a white Belfast sink with two wooden draining boards and a walk-in pantry with a white tiled shelf. A built-in glass fronted dresser with drawers and cupboards underneath; a gas freestanding cooker with a plate rack, and a scullery that had a deep white Belfast sink with a washboard. I do not know how my mother reached the sink; she must have stood on a stool, as she was a tiny lady, not even 5ft tall. Both sinks had hot and cold-water taps. The hot water came from the back boiler in the fireplace during the wintertime. An immersion heater, situated in the airing cupboard in the back bedroom, supplied our hot water during the summertime. Our new kitchen addition was the blessing of a "Copper". A Copper was a large copper drum, powered by gas at its base, which Mother only used for the cleaning of our "whites". Mother would fill with cold water and add Persil washing powder, once dissolved she would add the linens and then bring to the boil. Once the laundry had reached the desired boiling stage, Mother would remove the laundry using a wooden tong with a metal handle and drag the linen into a bowl, then take to the sink for rinsing. On the last cold rinse, Mother would add a "dolly blue bag" to enhance her whites. Every day when I came home from school, there pegged up, was a line of washing, held up with a prop blowing in the wind from one end of the garden to the other. It was a very long garden. All of the bedrooms had built in cupboards and fireplaces with a tiled surround, shelf and hearth. There was an upstairs toilet, no more pots, and a separate small bathroom.

Example of our freestanding gas cooker. Next to the cooker is an example of our Copper

On display at The Poole Museum 2018.

Although money was still short, things were much nicer in this house. We had very good neighbours in the whole road whereby we would all help each other. Many a time my parents would send me to the neighbours to either, borrow a cup of sugar; a loaf of bread; or even a shilling for the gas and the neighbours did the same also. My mother made rugs out of old woollen coats by cutting strips of cloth, all colours, then weaving them into an old clean piece of sack. One of the rugs, Mother wrote the words "Home" and placed it by the front door. They lasted for years. Every week my mother would scrub all the floors on her knees. All the handles to open the windows were brass, and as such, my mother used Brasso to clean the handles and Windolene for the glass. Nevertheless, things did get much better, as my eldest sister, now 15 years old, was working at the Corona factory in West Quay Road Poole, to help pay towards her keep. My eldest sister also helped Mother quite a lot with the cleaning of the house.

The garden was a corner plot, so quite large with a mass of prickles and weeds. My father set about clearing the ground, which was very hard work. Much later he planted potato cut offs to clear the soil. We also kept chickens so my father did not need fertiliser. A while later he started to plant fruit trees; fruit bushes; cabbages to name but a few and runner beans from his own dried beans as seeds were very hard to come by. Most people of Poole did try and grown their own food and an allotment scheme was set up at Baiter Park for those with limited space. Before my mother cooked the dinner, she would put on her Wellington boots and venture into the garden to dig up the food for dinner, and we girls would collect the fruit for her pies. I can still remember those golden drop gooseberries, as sweet as honey! Not like today's sour as "old nick"! I can also remember the rhubarb it grew so tall in the summertime. My father grew salad vegetables too, lettuces, cucumbers, spring onions and tomatoes. No greenhouse just sheets of glass.

It's Getting Better

Life progressed on; I had a childhood, no money, but lots of friends. As I write I start to chuckle to myself, remembering that our dad used to put a basin on our heads to cut our hair, as we could not afford to go to the hairdressers. Afterwards, Mother would tie a big white bow of ribbon on one side of your head. Due to the weight of the bow, your head was lopsided. Some fortunate girls at school were lucky enough to have bows on either side of their heads, which levelled out their heads.

Our house was an open door. Things went back to normal. Dad continued to work and I went back to school, albeit a little bit older now. There was no such thing as housing benefit back then, you had to work or starve. However, there was child allowance, about twenty-five shillings a child, but nothing for the first child, and a clothing allowance for school. This did help us financially given there was more rent to pay.

We still played on the quay. I can remember, (grinning to myself as I write) my brother was walking down the slipway for the lifeboat at fishermen's dock. When, my brother slipped on the green slime, my older sister hastening to grab his hair, just in time, and pulling him out of the dock by his head. Oh happy days! Generally this was a "no play zone" as the lifeboat could come rushing out for an emergency at any given time and not too mention, obviously extremely dangerous.

My youngest sister started school, the second eldest started work at fifteen, and one-by-one we all grew up in our home and went to work which made it a lot easier for my mother and father.

We eventually all married one by one and left home; mind you, do you ever leave home? My parents never left that house or Poole for that matter and eventually bought the house sometime later. That house was always full of grandchildren, relatives and friends and it is still in the family today and remains to be full. My father died of a heart attack when he was only 77. However, my mother continued to live in that house until she was 99½ and died of old age.

Ration Books

They seemed to go on for some time after the war had ended and my mother continued to use the same grocery store. It was Chas Laughtons at the end of Coles Avenue in Hamworthy. We had eight ration books, one per person in each household. When you ordered your groceries every week, they cut the points out of your books. When the points were gone, you could not have any more food, even if you had the money to buy more. Everyone received the same amount of points each for a product every week. So for instance, if your allowance was 1oz of tea per person, per week and we had eight in our family, we got 8oz's of tea and the grocer cut out 1 point from each book. This ensured that you could not buy any more from any other shop. Therefore, Mother had to make sure we did not run out of tea or you were on the Bev coffee for the rest of the week. Accordingly, if you used your 8oz's of margarine, you were on the dripping. Sometimes my mother would be able to get half a pigs head or pigs trotters from the butcher and cook for my father's supper. He used to sit in the kitchen at the table, slice off a piece, and eat it with bread. He loved it! Sometimes I would fetch chitterlings or sweetbreads, as they were a cheap cut of pork no doubt.

Swapping

The neighbours helped each other. If you kept chickens, and we did, we swapped our eggs for flour, or for whatever items we needed, no money was ever exchanged, only goods.

Growing up in Poole

It was not all play as a young child! There were many corner shops in Poole and from a very young age, my mother and grandmother sent me on errands. Not for much, as I was only little and we did not have many pennies.

As I got a little older, my chores became more responsible and further afield. One was to pay the grocery bill and give the next week's order. Mr Laughton used to deliver the groceries to my gran's house and leave the bill. When I went to his shop to pay the bill, he always gave me a tube of Rowntree's fruit gums for coming. My mother was busy, as always.

My Gran

*W*as getting older and her legs were not that good. No rest homes then, you looked after your own elderly relatives. I should think it was because of all the scrubbing she has had to do on those knees. In South Road, next to the school, was a drill hall for the army. On many occasions, I saw my grandmother on her knees washing the floor, must have seemed an endless job, as the floor was huge and no doubt, only to have been paid a few pence.

Gran's House

*F*or my Saturday job, I used to go to my gran's house every Saturday at 9 am sharp! There my gran stood waiting on the front doorstep for me as I walked up the road to greet her.

My grandmother and grandfather lived on South Road, which was at the end of our lane. At the bottom of my gran's garden was Lagland Street County Primary (infant) School. She used to stand on her doorstep and watch me in the playground at playtime. At the front of my gran's house, she had South Road School. Gran's house was in a terrace of houses with an alleyway between them to share and it had an attic for me to play in. Her house was similar to our old house, but her house had three bedrooms and had two sets of very narrow stairs to climb. It was in much better condition than ours was. In her sitting room, they had a large Welsh dresser fitted to the wall with lots of pretty china upon it. Also, a cheese dish and a glass cake stand along with other bits and bobs. I think Grandad must have brought them back for her when on his travels in the Navy. They did have eight children, all born in Poole, all had flown the nest, but they still did visit occasionally. Gran was a great royalist, many coronation mugs hung on the dresser and photos of the royal kings and queens back to Queen Victoria, which hung in every room, even in the attic. I wonder what she would think of the Royal Family now. Her mahogany sideboard was a plethora of family photo frames. They had 8 children and 14 grandchildren then. In the corner of the room, by the window, stood a table with a cloth covering it, on which was the radio, mainly to hear the world news and weather forecasts and always the church services on Sunday. She used to get out her bible to follow the service, as she did not go to church now, as she was unable to stand for long periods. The radio worked by an accumulator. I used to take this to Stones in the High Street to be "charged up", and to pick up another, it cost sixpence. The shop was lovely. My grandparents both used to listen to the news on the radio, as televisions were a luxury item only the wealthy could own, not to mention, you needed electricity and there was no electricity in Gran's house. There was a black leather "chaise" lounge daybed under the window; a large square table in the centre of the room covered in a pretty cloth; an armchair and a wooden recliner for grandad, which he used to sit in and smoke his pipe. There were also three wooden wheeled backed chairs, on which you would often find Gran's tabby cat sitting on. Sometimes the cat used to spring up and try to knock the cage with my gran's budgie in, off the wall, he never could. Talk about Tom & Jerry. Gran used to throw her slipper at him. The small window had a tortoiseshell pole with chenille curtains. Her fireplace was of black wrought iron, that I used to polish with Zebo black polish until it shone. She always had a lovely fire in the wintertime, as there was no central heating then.

The drill hall for the soldiers, during the war, was across the road next to South Road School. There were dances held in the hall for the servicemen, probably the American soldiers too, although I would not have known the difference. I could see and hear them if I stood on a box on tiptoe from my grandmother's attic window at night. Of course, my gran did not know I was doing this, as I was supposed to be fast asleep. In the attic, stood against the wall, were pictures of beautiful ladies with long flowing hair, very Victorian. I do not know what happened to them, would love to have had them now. Whilst I was on my "attic room" adventures, I can remember finding a tin, being the curious creature that I was; I opened the tin and found some cake inside and as I was very hungry, I ate it. In the morning, I told my gran what I had done, and she said that it was a wedding cake and was 20 years old. Undoubtedly, the cake was clearly very well preserved, as it did not kill me! So much for today's "best before" dates.

The Major and his wife along with their two children were my gran's neighbours, lovely people. A delayed action bomb dropped in my gran's back garden; it made a hell of a noise and shattered her windows. Thankfully, no one was seriously hurt although my grandad had received cuts to his hands from the window glass and my uncle Harry's bike ended up two streets away. They used to sit in the pantry under the stairs when the sirens went off.

The Visits

There was not a bathroom in my gran's house as the lavatory was out in the yard next to the coalhouse, as was her tin bath, up on the fence. All the bedrooms in gran's house had a washstand that had a marble top with a towel holder. Placed on the top of the washstand were a very large china bowl and a jug, a very pretty and Victorian set with either roses or violets on them for hot water, along with a soap dish and toothbrush holder. Beneath the washstand, in a little cupboard, was a pot with a handle to go underneath the beds, all matching sets. When my aunt and uncle visited, my gran would ask me to fetch her very best linens from a metal tin chest in her bedroom, along with her Whitney blankets, which were as soft as silk.

The Cottage Garden

After the war, on the outside wall, under the kitchen window were the most beautiful white roses growing up it. Anytime we had a pot of tea, my gran would ask me to pour the spent leaves at the base of the rose bush to mulch the roses. I could not understand then, how anything so beautiful could grow out of such a small hole, of course, I do now, being that I am an avid gardener. The roots travelled under the bricks of the yard. I wonder, is that why some roses are called Hybrid Tea Roses now? Of course, I am only joking, as I know the real reason why they are named Hybrid Tea Roses. On the sill under the sitting room window was a trough with pots of blood red Chrysanthemum's. The small garden had a mixture of flowers and shrubs in it, including a rhubarb plant with a bucket over the top to force the rhubarb to grow.

Where my gran's house would have stood today. South Road – 2018.

The Women of Poole

Were a very proud bunch! No front garden, only a step straight onto the street, and this step was scrubbed white each week or polished with Cardinal Red. If your house had a brass doorknocker, you cleaned it to a high shine with Brasso. My gran even had a window cleaner who came on a bike, carrying his ladder and bucket. You filled his bucket with some water and he cleaned your windows and charged you about 3d. The windows in the streets during the winter times were very dirty, mainly from all of the coal smoke fires.

The Community

*I*t was great! They all helped each other, if they had a loaf of bread and you did not have any, they would give you half of it until payday. The cobbler would mend your shoes, the dressmaker your clothes and you found a way to help them in return. They all knew each other in Poole.

There were; to name but a few;

The Doctor – Adams
The Grocer – Mr Laughton
The Postman – Mr Harry Reeves
The Milkman – Mr Cross
The Coal Man – Mr Foster
The Publican – Mr & Mrs Elsom
The Teacher – Mr Francis
The Neighbours – The Army Major and his family & Mrs Toms.

Mrs Toms

*M*rs Toms was your typical Coronation Street type character. She used to pop round to my gran's house every weekday mornings, for a gossip and to see if my gran needed anything. Just knocked on the door and walked straight in calling out for my gran, "You hoo, Mrs Fisher" you would hear her call. They never locked their doors in the daytime then; Mrs Toms would still have her round curlers in her hair, held in by a hair turban.

The Coal Man – Mr Foster – Whittey's Coal Yard, Lagland Street.

*H*e usually came with his horse and cart. If there were manure left in the road, I would get a bucket and a shovel, pick it up, and put it on Gran's roses in her back garden. I did the same when Mr Cross, the milkman, came with his horse and cart too. Occasionally, Mr Foster would run out of coal from his yard and would be unable to deliver to my gran. Therefore, Gran would say, "Go down the road and borrow a cart from Royston, go to the coal house on the quay, and get half a hundredweight, a sack full" and gave me the money to pay for it. Coal used to come in off the boats into the coal house, which was where the Thistle Hotel on the quay is now situated. Remember I was only nine or ten years old and a skinny little girl. First, I made us both a hot cup of Camp coffee; afterwards, I would head off to get the cart from Royston and wobbled it off to the coal shed. I remember it was big and dark inside. A man came and said, "Place the sack on the iron scales" when full, he lifted the heavy sack onto the cart for me and I paid him. Then I pushed the heavy cart squeaking back to Grans, but it was not too far. I did this most weeks on Saturday's. When Mr Foster did deliver, he would carry the sack on his back and then empty the sack straight into the coalhouse next to the outside toilet. On occasion, I would sometimes go to the coke yard near Fishermen's Dock, where the coke would come down a chute. At one time I could not borrow the cart as Royston was out, but I still went to the coke yard with my sack, thinking that I could carry a hundredweight, silly me! Luckily, a kind man offered to put it on his cart and walked me back to Gran's house. That is what people were like in Poole then.

Regardless of where or how I went to fetch the coal, Gran would always make sure I had a treat when I got back. Gran would say, "Go to Steels the bakery, on the corner and get three very hot jam doughnuts". I speedily took the cart back to Royston's and proceeded to head to the bakery, hardly being able to contain the excitement. When you opened the door, you could smell the baking bread. The shopkeeper gave me the large hot doughnuts in a brown paper bag, fresh out of the pan, oozing with jam, they cost 3d.

The Weekly Shop – The High Street.

First, I had to pick up the accumulator for the wireless and had to be careful not to spill it, luckily Gran only lived a stone's throw from Stones the shop.

Gran had made a shopping list, but I could not carry it all at once, so had to go back and forth several times. The High Street was buzzing; the shops all knew me as Gran Fisher's granddaughter.

On the corner of Carters Lane and the High Street, there was Miles a lovely haberdashery store. Coles the jewellery shop was across the street. Boons the hardware store was on the corner of Westons Lane, a very old hardware store. Across the road from it was Lookers a good stationer. It was a pleasure to shop in Poole High Street back then.

The Butchers – Dewhurst or Eastman's.

The floor, covered in sawdust; they had a big chopper, chopping block and smile. You could get a Sunday joint, a whole shoulder of lamb for 10 shillings, and you paid at the kiosk on your way out. It was enough for two days.

The High Street – source; The Poole Museum.

The Bakers – Hoares or Steels.

The doors were always open and you could see the bakers inside baking the bread. The smell was gorgeous! Not sliced or in plastic wrap like today. You always had to queue.

The Fishmongers – Mac Fisheries.

I used to get a pint of winkles for Gran on Saturdays. They had everything laid out fresh on the slab; you could pick your own. Sometimes we would have a crab for Saturday tea, "Oh and 3 pennies worth of catfish please"! I asked, which I cooked for the cat, it stank the kitchen out. You paid at the kiosk on the way out.

Millers Pie Shop

Oh, the smell of those hams and pies! Mmmm, and the sausages, all varieties hung up on hooks, they were out of this world. The shopkeeper sliced your ham off the bone and covered in breadcrumbs for about 2 shillings a quarter. They had a factory in Poole where many of the young people went to work when they left school at fifteen.

The Chemist – Boots and Timothy Whites.

The Grocery Shops – Pearks, Lipton's, Burdens and World Stores.

Can you believe shops like these? They cut everything, sliced everything, they weighed it, priced it, wrapped it and bagged it. You purchased your tea, sugar and even dried fruit in this way also. The butter, cheese and lard were in big blocks on a cooled tile shelf. The cheese smelt heavenly. The shopkeeper only cut off, using a wire, the amount you needed. We never experienced food wastage, there was not such a thing, especially where food was concerned, unlike what we see today! No ready sealed packets! No plastic packaging! Just thick paper bags.

The Shoe Shop – Hawkes.

My gran joined a boot club for me at Hawkes. I paid sixpence a week. When I needed shoes and had enough in my book, they would measure my feet. It was one pound ten shillings for school shoes or two pounds for Sunday bests, namely Clarks shoes. It was nice not to go to school with holes in the bottoms of my shoes. In the summer, I wore brown leather sandals, they smelt lovely, a nice change from Wellington boots.

The Sweet Shop – Stokes.

Situated at the end of Green Road opposite The Foundry Arms pub. The sweet jars were from floor to the ceiling, all the traditional varieties; sherbet lemons that made your eyes water; bullseyes; clove balls; winter mixture; aniseed balls; Cadbury's chocolate buttons; barley sugar sticks and all shapes of liquorice, to name but a few. The choices were endless. Of course, when rationing books were in operation, you could only buy 2oz a week, which made it very difficult to know which sweet to choose? The shopkeeper had to stand on a stool to reach the jars; he or she would then weigh them on the little silver scales and tip them into a white paper bag. You were on cloud nine when you walked away, but soon the daunting realisation knowing that they had to last you all week, some hope!

The Ice Cream Man – Luigi.

He was Italian. Luigi would come along on his bicycle and would ring his bell. You took a bowl or a jug out to him and he filled it with the most wonderful ice cream. Luigi made the ice cream using unpasteurised dairy ingredients, and no preservatives or additives either, unheard of today!

The Fishing Boats

Sometimes, Gran would send me along to the quay to wait for the fishing boats to come in with fresh Sprats from the sea. They used to give them to me free if they had loads to take home with them. You needed quite a few because they were only tiny. Gran would coat the Sprats in flour and fry them, serving them with bread and butter for tea and seasoned nicely with a sprinkling of pepper.

Clothes Shops

There were some lovely ones in the High Street. If you had the money it was Marks & Spencer's, if not, then it was Woolworths as they were very cheap. Marks and Spencer's a little further down the High Street, had everything laid out on the counters, with an assistant on each counter providing you with a personal service, unlike today. You could buy a fully-fashioned cardigan or jumper in beautiful colours for one pound ten shillings each, the cost of which you could also buy baby dresses at Woolworths. There was also a big Bonmarché, it was a lovely store then. It sold everything, not just clothes, and at Christmas time, they had a Father Christmas upstairs. Kashmir's too, which was a lovely smart shop for women, you could buy a lovely dress for £4 and a beautiful coat for £9 and Fifty Shilling Tailors for men's clothing.

The Railway Box

It was by the bridge and the railway line gates in Poole High Street. In my time, these gates were hand operated. There was a man in a little box on the left hand side, next to the now estate agents. He used to turn a big wheel after ringing a bell if a train was to come. There were two single gates for the public to cross, one each side of the lines. When we saw a train coming, we would watch the smoke from the top of the bridge, phew! The boys took down the train number and we all went home smelling of smoke, that pleased our mothers!

The Greengrocer – Moores.

I bought Gran's potatoes, covered in dirt, from Moores market. I had to go back to get another 5lbs because they were too heavy for me to carry all in one go. On one side was fruit and on the other were vegetables. You picked up your own; the shopkeeper weighed them, packed in brown paper bags and placed straight in your sack bag. No plastic carrier bags then!

Gran gave me some pocket money for doing all her shopping, usually a two-shilling piece. On Saturday afternoon's I went to the cinema (we called it "going to the pictures" in my day), The Amity, for the matinee film, or, as the locals aptly named it, "The Flea Pit". You paid sixpence for the film and I usually had enough left for a bag of sweets. In most instances, they were showing Roy Rogers or a film with cowboys and Indians. After the pictures, I went back to my gran's house for tea before going home.

In my grans garden, growing all along a wire fence was a loganberry bush, similar to raspberries, only twice as big and delicious. I used to get a small basin and pick them for our tea, which we had with Carnation milk yum! We could not have cream as my gran did not have a fridge. Gran served them with bread, fresh that day (crusty) and butter or as an alternative, and only on occasion, but not often, a slice of homemade cake, seedy cake or Madeira cake, if my gran did not have any dried fruit to make a fruit cake with.

The Pubs

There were many pubs in Poole and on the Quay. At one-time a relative of mine was the landlord of The Portsmouth Hoy. Back then, the locals considered pubs to be a place for a break after a hard day's work, nowadays it is a social place. As a young child, if I saw any empty beer bottles lying around the streets and alleyways, I would collect them to take back to the pub they came from and then the pub would pay me a few pennies for returning them. As there were many pubs in Poole at that time, it was a way for us children to earn a little extra pocket money.

The Pub Run

On Saturday's, before going home, my gran sent me to collect some Fetal for her. I had to go to Mr and Mrs Elsom's, who were the publicans (tenants) at "The London" which was my gran's local pub in Lagland Street. You had to take your own small bottle and pay sixpence. Fetal was similar to Ginger Beer, hot in spice, but certainly not for children! It was Mr and Mrs Elsom's own home brew. They served me at the bottle and jug entrance, and yes, at 10 years old! I can remember looking in through to the "Public Bar" which was noisy and full of smoke. Sometimes there were darts matches going on in the "lounge bar". The London is still there today but now called the Cockleshell Pub. My gran also liked Stout and had it with her supper of cheese and bread. My uncle Harry worked for the Brewers Eldridge Pope, so he would often bring Stout home for her.

Usually, my father sent me to the pub on a Saturday evening to fetch beer for him. You had to take back your empty bottles or jug, and then the publican would refill them from the draught, choosing either light or brown ale.

The Portsmouth Hoy, 2018.

The Cockleshell Pub, 2018.

Christmas Time 1946-1950

We always had a traditional Christmas; we still had the glow and warmth of a fire in the hearth and what a welcome it was on a cold and frosty December night after an evening of carol singing. We kids went carol singing with a used cocoa tin with the hope of collecting a few pennies to buy a little Christmas shopping. We used to start at the beginning of December, but Christmas Eve was when we received the most, as by then most people were in the spirit of Christmas.

The prep before Christmas was always a very exciting time with Dad making the Christmas puddings in a large china bowl with a wooden spoon. First, he would prepare the basins and white cloths for steaming. He always added beer and lastly a silver Victorian sixpence. All of us children, stood around watching him make the Christmas puddings hoping to lick the bowl afterwards and then wondering who was going to be the lucky one this year to find the sixpence?

We always had a real tree. Firstly, we would cover a bucket with something Christmassy or red crepe paper and plant the tree in some soil, so it would not drop its needles all over the floor. Years ago, the *poor* people did not have carpets in their houses. Even my gran did not have carpets in her house, only Lino that you would get on your knees and polish using Mansion polish, plain or lavender scented, smelt lovely! The tree was quite big, had several wide branches, and went in the corner of the sitting room. My eldest sister would start the decorations on the tree with lots of small fairy lights. I remember all the colours and how it would twinkle. We children would continually add to the tree decorations right up until Christmas Eve with the decorations we had made in school and sweets we could tie on. We could not sleep due to all the excitement. As for the trimmings, we made our own then, with lots of paper chains and crepe paper cut into thin strips, all colours. They were twisted and placed across the ceiling, held up with drawing pins. Then would come the blowing up of the balloons, all shapes even sausage ones. We would tie the balloons together and then we would place them in the corners of the room and put silver tinsel all over the trimmings making them look very festive, how it shone!

We each had a Christmas stocking to hang up around the fire to be filled *"by someone"* (perhaps Santa) on Christmas Eve. The Christmas stockings were not the expensive readymade ones that you see in the shops nowadays, oh no! They were my mother's clean stockings or Dad's long socks. What a surprise to see them hanging on Christmas morning and filled up. All day we would treasure our stockings full of treats.

Our presents were in pillowcases placed at the bottom of our beds ready for when you awoke on Christmas morning along with the sound of the cockerel crowing; well at least he was not our Christmas dinner! The gifts we received were made with love; we young girls had little dolls dressed by our mother and toys to treasure. These gifts did not cost a fortune, but then, my parents did not have a fortune and at that time, I still believed in Father Christmas. Along with our toys were nuts to crack, an orange and Rowntree's fruit pastilles. Our friends would be knocking at the door asking us what "what did you get?" and sharing with each other, then off running around the road to see all of our friends too, wishing all that we saw along the way a Merry Christmas.

Christmas time was the <u>only time</u> we ever had an orange and oh my, what a treat it was, you certainly knew it was Christmas. Fruit was a rare treat and certainly no bananas! Unlike today, most children have an orange or a banana in their lunchboxes and eat fruit on a daily basis. During the war years, banana ships or other food supplies from foreign countries could not get through to England. These ships were in great danger of being torpedoed or attacked from the air, although our Armed Forces did a good job trying to prevent this, and our Royal Navy did their very best in escorting the ships through, albeit in great danger themselves.

On Boxing Day, we three youngest girls went to my auntie Violets (we called her Aunt Vie) and Uncle Peter's house in Poole. My aunt Violet was my mother's sister; they only had one child a little girl named Sandra. Even now, 70 years later, I cannot pass that house without remembering the wonderful times and the laughter we had with them all on Boxing Days. Aunt's Gladys and Aunt Jess, my mother's older two sisters, used to join us as well. The atmosphere around their tree, again a real one, was intense. I remember it being very large with lights and crackers. My uncle Peter dressed up as

Father Christmas and a round-barrel one at that, he was great at it. The Christmas tea Auntie Vie made was lovely, with homemade trifle containing real fruit and jelly, accompanied by a Christmas cake with candles on, all glowing in the dark. Then came the presents. Every year we each received the same presents, mainly underwear, vests and knickers, petticoats with frills on the bottom, yes, we wore them then, all purchased from Marks and Spencer's. These would be a great help to my mother towards our school clothing costs. We also received a little toy and always a bar of chocolate.

Speaking of toys, I remember my dad giving me a big china doll with a thick elastic band running through its middle that hooked the head, arms and legs altogether. The trouble was they kept coming off and it was hard for my little fingers to hook them back on. Therefore, I usually walked around with a doll with something missing, but I did not mind, after all, I had a doll and that was good enough for me. My only brother had a big red train and a grey bomber plane. To the annoyance of my mother, he would go running around the house making a heck of a noise.

My Grandparents

They lived and died in Poole, as did generations before them. My grandfather was born in East Street and my grandmother, Lagland Street (considered the most overpopulated road in Poole). They had another seven children all born in Poole. Well, they never had a TV in those days.

My grandfather, a retired seaman, died first in 1947, aged 81. My grandmother went on to live another 11 years and died in her house in Poole at the grand old age of 86 in 1958, I was 18. The postman, Mr Reeves was a lovely man; I can see his smile now. He used to collect her pension for her from the post office and said to me what a "Grand Lady" she was. She always changed her frock in the afternoon and did her hair, which was a long plait, even at her age. It went around her head. Mr Reeves was also the postman (on a bicycle) that delivered the mail to Mrs Christy on Brownsea Island. Now that is a lovely island to visit. My gran's milkman, Mr Cross, who came by horse and cart, used to bring a newspaper in for her every morning. She bought every one including The Daily Herald and read them all with accompanying magazines, such as My Friend and Woman's Own. She always had a neat pile on her table. Her neighbour used to take into my gran a Sunday dinner covered in a white cloth, a roast, straight from her oven.

Sometime later, the whole road of houses in South Road had to be demolished and council flats built up in their place. It was a good and bad change! Good because of the terrible environmental situations the community of people were living in, but bad because, when all of the properties were demolished, along went with it, was the community of Poole.

Changes & Conclusion

Baiter

*T*oday was a lovely day, so I decided to take a walk along Poole Quay; the tourists have yet to arrive, so it was not too overcrowded. I still have very strong legs. I walked from the shoreline at Baiter to Poole Bridge and back again. A very enjoyable walk this was. Along my journey, I must have passed several different nationalities. Yes, I can recall thinking Poole has definitely changed!

Fishing nets at Baiter – 2018.

*T*here were American soldiers in Poole during the war and they stayed in huts along Baiter and on the Quay. What is the saying? "There's many a man holding another man's baby, believing it to be his own". The American soldiers used to give out sweets to the children.

As I walked along, I came across "The Old Powder House". The Old Powder house used to be a stone building, which is where the gunpowder for the old sailing ships was stored. Keeping the gunpowder in this building protected the town from an explosion. Sadly, the building no longer remains but evidence of its existence remains today. I have reason to believe that The Society for Poole is trying to get a preservation order on the remains of this iconic site, before it completely disappears, as part of the Poole Heritage. I do hope they succeed at this.

The Old Powder House – 2018.

Shoreline at Baiter – 2018.

Changes to Poole

I knew Poole before the erection of the Arndale shopping centre. As the Hants and Dorset buses approached Poole, by The George Hotel, on their left and right were shops. Nice ones, like Southern and Northern Stores, a photographers shop, a dentist, Advance Laundry shop, a lovely fish and chip shop, a pet shop, a hardware shop, a butchers, a linen shop, a chemist, a shoe shop, a shoe repair shop, the Regent cinema and a newsagent.

The bus then turned left towards Poole Park and The Ladies' walking field. The Ladies Walking Field is now where Seldown Bridge and the Dolphin swimming centre are situated. Burdens the grocer was on its right, and what a lovely store too, the bus stopped at Ladies' walking field so you could go and do your shopping in the High Street.

Another bus went on and turned into Kingland Crescent by the gates and stopping after having passed many other shops including two pubs, a hotel, Poole Drapers, a sports shop, and two newsagents. These businesses were all demolished to make way for a bus station and The Arts Centre.

Now I can see more changes to Kingland Crescent, Poole Pottery, Corkers, and a gigantic block of flats by the George Hotel and in Lagland Street, more construction, two more blocks of flats. There is also vacant land by the train station and on the Quay next to the Thistle Hotel showing signs of a development.

To follow is just a snippet of photographs that I have taken of the ongoing changes around Poole.

Proposed Building works ongoing – 2017/2018

Vacant land adjacent to the Thistle Hotel on Poole Quay.

Previously Corkers restaurant on Poole Quay.

Kingland Crescent.
Soon to be demolished to make way for new cinema complex.

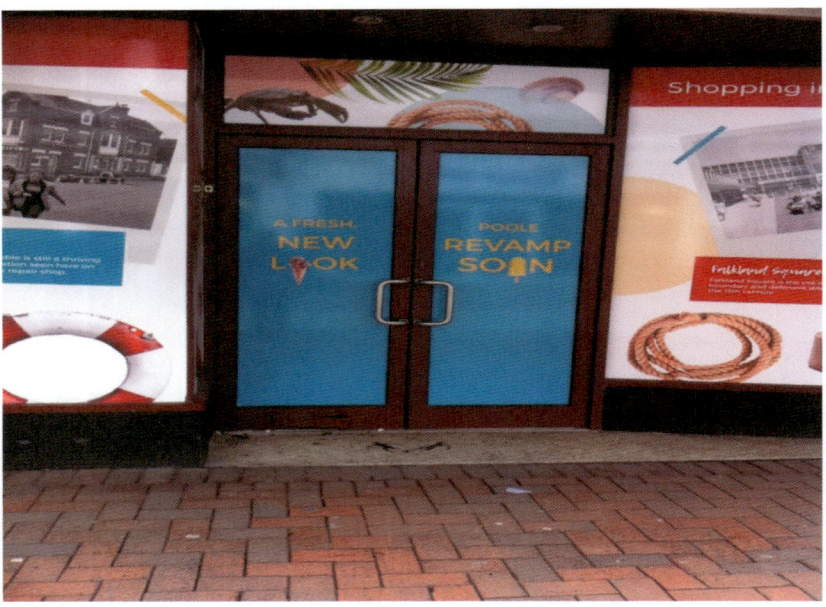

High Street North (both images).

65 | Memoirs of A Child in Poole

Globe Lane
(Before renovations).

Below – Globe Lane
(Completed 2018).

The Swimming Baths

At one time, there was an open-air swimming pool, now superseded with an indoor pool, near Poole Park with changing rooms. The train from Poole train station ran on the track beside it and we used to wave at the passengers on board when it passed by. The pool had a high diving board and it would cost 3d for entry.

Poole Park

We kids spent a lot of time there; after all, it did not cost any money. We used to walk from our home; it was lovely by the lakes. They sold lovely ice creams in the park, but we did not have any money to spend. Mum gave us bottled tap water and some jam sandwiches each to keep us going throughout the day.

A Change for the Better

You could not get to Baiter then from Poole Park, only at the Whitecliff end. Now after a lot of landfilling, you can get to Baiter via a pedestrian underpass and what a pleasure it is to walk along the shore to Fishermen's Dock where the fishermen hung their nets. When I was small, I used to see my grandfather there in his navy blue jumper and hat. He loved the quay, being a seaman. Moreover, where have all our large Poole cockles gone? I loved them!

A Good Change

I am glad to see that they have refurbished the old lifeboat house and made it into a museum with the old lifeboat inside. I have no doubt that this refurbished building will stand in good stead for another hundred years.

Lifeboat Museum – 2018.

Other Good changes.

I like the new mariner, especially the Sunseeker yachts, fabulous! Makes you feel like you could be in St Tropez, France. The Boat tours from the quay are truly wonderful. I regularly, in the spring and summertime's, take boat trips over to Brownsea Island for visits and enjoy the Wareham River cruises.

Sunseeker boats, Poole Quay 2018.

Below - The new Mariner 2018.

Poole Harbour Boat Cruises – 2018.

My Conclusion – At least for now.

Growing up in the poor conditions of Poole during the war years, gave me the strength of character to overcome the many obstacles that came my way, like bringing up a large family on my own, six children in fact! However, I am pleased to say that they have all turned out very well. As a child, although things were tough, I felt safe and happy.

As suggested to me that day, I have opened my eyes and taken a hard good look around at "Our Poole", and I must admit that I am pleasantly surprised. I very much like the changes to the quayside, with the boats taking pride of place and fisherman's dock. This is a very interesting area for both the old and the young. Baiter Park has been beautifully arranged for all to enjoy, including the dogs. With the ever-changing scenery, you never tire of sitting there to rest on one of the many seats, after a leisurely stroll. In addition, Poole Park with its distant views, very pleasing, and the changes to the Old Town, St James area, remarkable. I remember how it smelt, in the good old days.

The newly refurbished Custom House, I would highly recommend and the new Poole Pottery Shop is definitely worth a visit. Not forgetting the Poole Museum; with their plethora of historical information a delightful coffee shop, accompanied by the spectacular views of the Poole Bay.

Overall, my thoughts on Poole Quay are very good. When I was growing up in Poole during the wartime, I felt secure, safe and happy, now that's odd, due to the fact that there were bombs dropping all around us and we were about to lose our home. However, we all had the support of our good friends and neighbours. What do the Poole people have today? I would conclude that I feel this is pretty much the census in most communities today. My conclusion is, yes, Poole is changing, but so are the times. Someone once asked me what I missed about Poole, and I replied "The smell and the community", both of which are now gone. However, this is not necessarily a sad matter, I am just learning to embrace all that is and has become today.

Printed in Great
Britain
by Amazon